MAR 2 2 20[ ]

D1242824

North America

by Rebecca Hirsch

Content Consultant
John I. Sharp, PhD.

Reading Consultant
Jeanne Clidas
Reading Specialist

Children's Press®
An Imprint of Scholastic Inc.
New York • Toronto • London • Auckland • Sydney • Mexico City
New Delhi • Hong Kong • Danbury, Connecticut

Library of Congress Cataloging-in-Publication Data
Hirsch, Rebecca E.
  North America / by Rebecca Hirsch.
     p. cm. – (Rookie read-about geography)
  Includes index.
  ISBN 978-0-531-28980-8 (lib.bdg.) – ISBN 978-0-531-29280-8
(pbk.)
  1. North America–Juvenile literature. 2. North
America–Geography–Juvenile literature. I. Title.

E38.5.H36 2012
970–dc23

                              2012013406

1 2 3 4 5 6 7 8 9 10 R 22 21 20 19 18 17 16 15 14 13

Photographs © 2013: Alamy Images: 4 (Ilene MacDonald), 10
(Richard Levine); Dreamstime/Francesca Braghetta: cover right inset;
iStockphoto/Jim Parkin: 22; Lance W. Clayton: 12; NASA: 29; National
Geographic Stock: 16, 31 top right (John Eastcott and Yva Momatiuk),
8 (John Scofield), 24, 31 bottom left (Skip Brown); Photo Researchers,
Inc./Thomas E. Evans: 18; Robert Fried Photography: cover left inset;
Shutterstock, Inc.: 30 (airn), 20, 31 bottom right (Jim Lopes), cover
(Orhan Cam); Superstock, Inc./Ambient Images Inc.: 14; Thinkstock/
iStockphoto: 26, 31 top left.

Map by Matt Kania/www.maphero.com

Table of Contents

Banff National Park, Alberta, Canada

4

Welcome to North America!

North America is the third largest continent in the world. It has big countries. It also has small countries and islands.

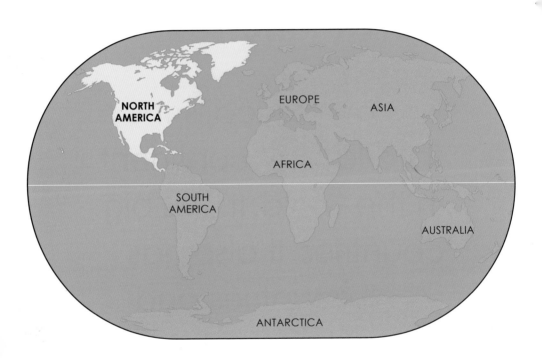

NORTH
AMERICA

EUROPE

ASIA

AFRICA

SOUTH
AMERICA

AUSTRALIA

ANTARCTICA

The largest pieces
of land on Earth are
continents. There are
seven. North America
is the yellow continent
on this map.

A Mayan woman makes corn tortillas.

People of North America

Native Americans were the first people in North America. Many still live there.

Schoolchildren visit a skyscraper
in New York City.

North Americans come from all over the world. Some live in large cities.

A farm in the United States

Some live in small towns or on farms.

Children watch a Chinese New Year parade.

New people bring their customs with them. They bring new foods, celebrations, and special holidays.

Moose grow a new pair of antlers each year.

Amazing Animals

North America has
many different animals.
Moose are large
animals that eat plants.

American alligators have between 74 and 80 teeth. Adult humans have 32 teeth.

American alligators
are great swimmers.
They live in swamps
and ponds.

Redwood trees in Sequoia National Park

Land and Water

North America has forests. These redwood trees are the tallest trees in the world.

Bison eating grass on the prairie

North America has prairies. Prairies are flat land with many kinds of grasses. Bison and prairie dogs live on prairies.

The Rocky Mountains

North America has
tall mountains where
people camp and hike.

A barge on the Great Lakes

North America has many lakes. Boats on the five Great Lakes bring coal and iron to the people of North America.

Modern Marvels

- The U.S. space shuttle Atlantis took astronauts to space.

- The launch pad was made of steel and concrete.

- Two rocket boosters pushed the shuttle up during lift-off.

- The orbiter had the crew, kitchen, and beds inside.

Try It!

What is the launch pad made of? How many rocket boosters are on the shuttle? If you built your own space shuttle, what would it have on the inside?

rocket boosters

orbiter

launch pad

29

Meet a Black Bear

- Black bears live in forests of North America.

- They are good at climbing trees.

- Bear cubs live with their mother for two years.

- Mother bears work hard to protect their cubs.

Words You Know

boat

moose

mountains

trees

Index

Facts for Now

Visit this Scholastic Web site for more information
on North America:
www.factsfornow.scholastic.com
Enter the keywords **North America**

About the Author

Rebecca Hirsch is a scientist-turned-writer and the
author of many books for young readers.